W9-ATT-760

Quahog State of Mind

Don Bousquet

Covered Bridge Press
North Attleborough, MA 02760

AUGUST HAS BEEN A TOUGH MONTH. EVERY ONE OF US WOULD HAVE PERISHED IF NOT FOR OUR INDIAN FRIENDS AND THEIR RECIPE FOR SQUID INK FETTUCCINE WITH MUSSELS...
THE RECORDINGS OF ROGER WILLIAMS
DON BOUSQUET

SELF-CLEANING COVEN

AFTER 38 YEARS, A SCARBOROUGH STATE
BEACH EMPLOYEE NEARS RETIREMENT

GOOD NEWS, SON! THE 'JOURNAL' NO LONGER REFERS TO YOU AS A 'CONVICTED FELON'..... YOU'RE NOW A 'REPUTED MOB FIGURE DOING TIME'.

"HEY, SKIPPER, THE NATIVES HERE TALK REAL FUNNY BUT THEY'RE FRIENDLY. ONE OF THEM OFFERED ME SOME VODKA AND ANOTHER RENTED ME THIS MOPED. CAN WE STAY SKIPPER, CAN WE?!"

DINING 'AL FRESCO' IN THE PARKING
LOT OF THE BURGER KING IN WAKEFIELD

" LISTEN, VINNY... EITHER SLOW DOWN OR PUT THE TOP UP ! "

SOUTH COUNTY TURF FARMER

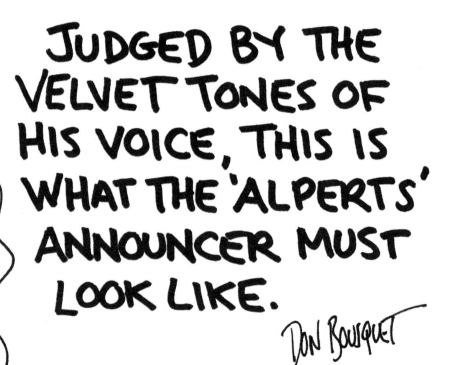

THE HUMPBACK OF NOTRE DAME

NOT EVERYONE KNOWS THERE WAS AN
AIRCRAFT CARRIER NAMED, 'BLOCK ISLAND'.
IT WAS QUITE SMALL.

"HERE'S YOUR BILL. WE FIGURE THIS HERE METAL ROD WAS YOUR PROBLEM. NEXT TIME YOUR HOOD WON'T CLOSE BRING HER IN AN' WE'LL RETRACT THAT BUGGER FOR YOU."

THIRD DAY OF ASCENT. TODAY WE WENT ON OXYGEN. VERY TIRED. HOPE TO SEE SUMMIT IN TWO MORE DAYS.

MUST CONFESS WE MAY HAVE BEEN FOOLISH IN ATTEMPTING TO SCALE THE NORTH FACE OF THE JOHNSTON LANDFILL.

THE UNFORTUNATE RESULT OF A
HOSTILE TAKEOVER IN PT. JUDITH

PONCE de LEON VISITS
RHODE ISLAND, 1514...

...AND DISCOVERS
"DA BUBBLA OF YOOT"

"IT's A TICKET FOR FIVE MILES
AN HOUR OVER THE LIMIT AND A
BUMPER STICKER THAT SAYS,' R.I.
TROOPERS : ALWAYS THERE WHEN YOU
NEED THEM'..."

IN THE ENGINE ROOM OF
THE BLOCK ISLAND BOAT

" WELL, MA'AM, TO BE PERFECTLY HONEST
THIS CAR IS PRETTY HEAVY AND KIND OF
LOUD. OUR MECHANIC SAYS IT PULLS REAL
HARD TO THE RIGHT AND THAT PROBLEM
CAN'T BE FIXED...
     AFTER ALL, IT IS A LIMBAUGHINI ! "

MANY THOUSANDS OF
RHODE ISLANDERS RECEIVED THEIR
DRIVER TRAINING FROM THIS MAN.

"PASSING IN THE BREAKDOWN LANE, SPEEDING THROUGH A CAUTION SIGNAL, FAILURE TO YIELD AT AN INTERSECTION... OKAY, PAL, GET OUT OF THE VEHICLE SLOWLY AND LET ME HAVE A LOOK AT THAT RHODE ISLAND DRIVER'S LICENSE!!"

SWAMP YANKEE IN ANALYSIS

WITH EQUANIMITY RHODE ISLAND
ACCEPTS THE FIRST STORM OF 1995

POINTY
JUDITH
COUNTRY
CLUB

OUR FOUNDER

STREET VENDORS LINED UP
OUTSIDE THE NEW MAIN OFFICE OF
THE REGISTRY OF MOTOR VEHICLES
IN PAWTUCKET.

"OUR SPEAKER TODAY HAS TAKEN
TIME FROM HIS BUSY SCHEDULE TO
TALK TO US ABOUT A REWARDING
CAREER AS A CASINO BOUNCER."

GARY LEY'S FORECAST OF ONE TO
TWO INCHES WAS BECOMING TRUE...
BUD STOOD THERE ON THE LOADING
DOCK CACKLING FIENDISHLY AS HE
REALIZED HE WAS ABOUT TO BECOME
A VERY WEALTHY MAN.

Editor's Note:

Just as Picasso had his "Blue Period," Don Bousquet has recently entered what may be known as his "Hair Club Period."

We are pleased to present a special section of eight Hair Club cartoons, suitable for framing, which demonstrate what can happen when an artist becomes fixated on a topic.

It is not known at this time when this period will end, but we at Covered Bridge Press remain guardedly optimistic.

MEMBER OF THE
HAIR CLUB STEAK FOR MEN

HAIR CLUB FOR SAILBOATERS MEMBER

WELL-TRAVELED ALIENS WHO'VE SPENT A LOT
OF TIME ABDUCTING RHODE ISLANDERS

RHODE ISLAND VAMPIRE-QUAHOGGER

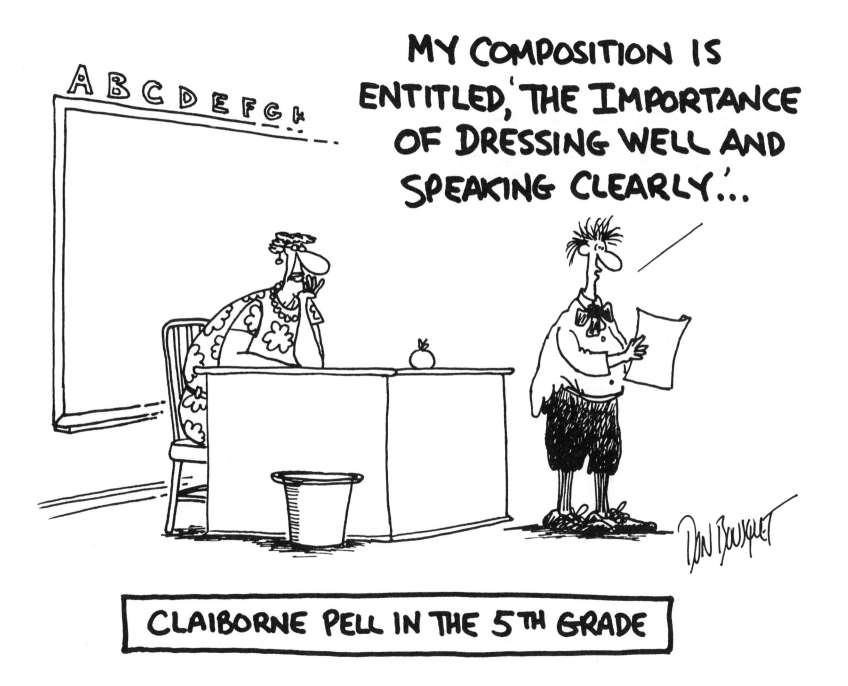

'SAVE THE BAY' REPORTS A SLOW BUT MEASURABLE IMPROVEMENT IN THE QUALITY OF UPPER NARRAGANSETT BAY MERMAIDS.

Don Bousquet

SUDDENLY, I CAST ASIDE MY RAKE,
REALIZING WHAT I MUST DO... I
WOULD SEEK THE SENATE SEAT OF
CLAIBORNE PELL!!

"THE JUICE" INTENSIFYS HIS SEARCH FOR
THE REAL KILLER(S) ON A GOLF COURSE IN FLORIDA